AN INCONVENIENT ALPHABET

Ben Franklin & Noah Webster's Spelling Revolution

For Lillian, Corinne, Paxton, and Everett,
and every student who passed through my classroom
—B. A.

To my sidekicks: Harry, Penny, and Franklin
—E. B.

SIMON & SCHUSTER BOOKS FOR YOUNG READERS

An imprint of Simon & Schuster Children's Publishing Division

1230 Avenue of the Americas, New York, New York 10020

Text copyright © 2018 by Beth Anderson

Illustrations copyright © 2018 by Elizabeth Baddeley

SIMON & SCHUSTER BOOKS FOR YOUNG READERS is a trademark of Simon & Schuster, Inc.

For information about special discounts for bulk purchases, please contact Simon & Schuster

Special Sales at 1-866-506-1949 or business@simonandschuster.com.

The Simon & Schuster Speakers Bureau can bring authors to your live event. For more information or to book an event, contact

the Simon & Schuster Speakers Bureau at 1-866-248-3049 or visit our website at www.simonspeakers.com.

Book design by Elizabeth Baddeley and Chloë Foglia • The text for this book was set in Caslon and hand-lettered.

The illustrations for this book were rendered using a mix of traditional and digital media.

Manufactured in China

1018 SCP

2 4 6 8 10 9 7 5 3

Library of Congress Cataloging-in-Publication Data

Names: Anderson, Beth, 1954– author. | Baddeley, Elizabeth, illustrator.

Title: An inconvenient alphabet : Ben Franklin and Noah Webster's spelling

revolution / Beth Anderson ; illustrated by Elizabeth Baddeley.

Other titles: Ben Franklin and Noah Webster's spelling revolution

Description: First edition. | New York : Simon & Schuster Books for Young

Readers, [2018] | "A Paula Wiseman Book." | Includes bibliographical references.

Identifiers: LCCN 2017061223 | ISBN 9781534405554 (hardcover) | ISBN 9781534405561 (eBook)

Subjects: LCSH: English language—United States—Orthography and spelling—Juvenile literature. | Spelling

reform—Juvenile literature. | Americanisms—Juvenile literature. | Webster, Noah, 1758–184—

Juvenile literature. | Franklin, Benjamin, 1706–1790—Juvenile literature.

Classification: LCC PE2817 .A53 2018 | DDC 428.1/3—dc23

LC record available at https://lccn.loc.gov/2017061223

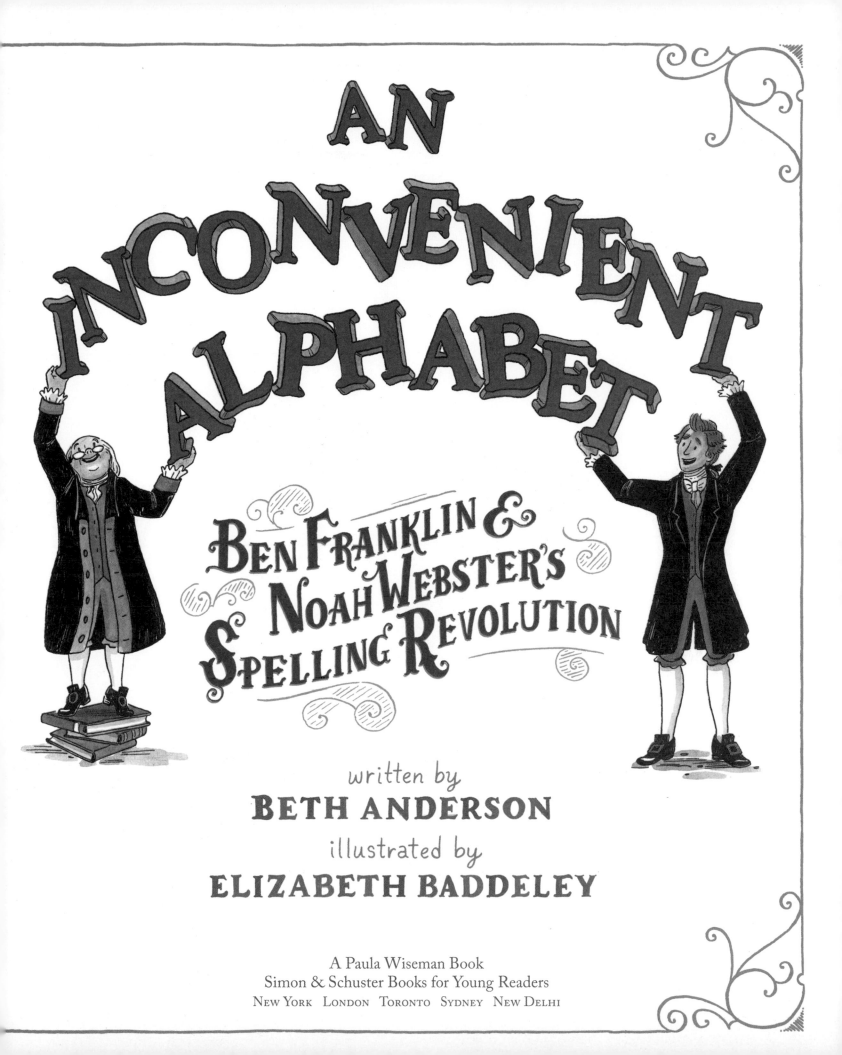

AN INCONVENIENT ALPHABET

BEN FRANKLIN & NOAH WEBSTER'S SPELLING REVOLUTION

written by

BETH ANDERSON

illustrated by

ELIZABETH BADDELEY

A Paula Wiseman Book
Simon & Schuster Books for Young Readers
NEW YORK   LONDON   TORONTO   SYDNEY   NEW DELHI

Y ou've probably heard of the American Revolution, when thirteen colonies rejected the rule of England. But there was another, much quieter, revolution in the colonies. . . .
Two men—
one old, one young,
both with big ideas—
battled an inconvenient alphabet.

Ben Franklin, a writer and printer, had no patience for people spelling words every which way. They should write the sounds they heard.

family or famely?

chair or chare?

write or writ?

letters or leters?

But how could anyone spell words correctly when letters didn't match sounds?
So Ben created a new alphabet.
He threw out *c, j, q, w, x,* and *y.*

He added *aw, uh, edh, ing, ish,* and *eth.*

DOG
DAG

UMBRELLA
YMBRELLY

FEATHER
FEHER

KING
KIŊ

FISH
FIh

TEETH
TEEh

Each letter had its own
sound—no more ABCs.

Ben shared his ideas and left them "to take their chance in the world."

When no one was interested in his alphabet, he tucked it away and focused on the business of the colonies.

The patriots declared independence from England. Armies
marched. Cannons boomed. When the war ended, the colonies
pulled together to form a nation.

But Americans from north to south and east to west couldn't understand one another. Some spoke like the king of England, others like backwoodsmen, and many barely spoke English at all.

Noah Webster, a writer and educator, had no patience for people pronouncing words every which way. They should say the sounds that were written. But how could anyone say words correctly when sounds didn't match letters?

BAITS) BEETS)

INE YON) ONION

YERB) HERB)

SPARROWGRASS) ASPARAGUS)

So Noah created a book to teach *American* English.
Grammar lessons.
Speaking instruction.
Page after page of pronunciation practice.
Noah hoped people would soon "converse together like children of the same family."

But Noah was a nobody. Some thought his voice squeaky and his
speeches boring. No one appreciated his work.
If only someone famous would join his efforts. Someone respected.
Someone the public adored.

Day after day, Noah traveled and lectured, selling his *Blue-Backed Speller*. Richmond, Baltimore, Dover.

In early 1786, Noah arrived in Philadelphia. More than anything, he needed to find support in the new capital, a city bustling with patriotism and promise. He called on publishers and governors, scientists and statesmen. He shared his ideas about American English. People listened and nodded.

But Noah hoped for more.

Finally, he arrived at the door of the most famous, most respected, most adored man in the city— Dr. Benjamin Franklin.

The two men spoke for hours about language and
education, about reading and writing.
Ben appreciated Noah's work.
Noah was interested in Ben's ideas.

Both agreed:
Some letters had too many sounds.

Some sounds had too many letters.

Some letters were just not needed at all.

The problem was the inconvenient alphabet.
Using twenty-six letters to write forty-four sounds caused nothing but trouble.

Pleased to find someone young and enthusiastic,
Ben dug out his old alphabet and dusted off his print blocks. Soon
every printer would need a set: new letter blocks to combine with
old ones to spell words in new ways. He gave them to Noah and
asked him to come up with a plan.

Energized by a partnership with Dr. Franklin, Noah set to work.
If letters matched sounds, you could read any word correctly.
If sounds matched letters, you could spell any word you heard.
Adding a few new letters, removing a few old ones,
Noah created a perfect alphabet.

BAITS

BEETS

ROXBER...

...PBERRY

INEYON

ONION

YERB

...SS ASPARAGUS

Noah sent Ben the plan—a new
alphabet for a new nation!
Ben approved.

PUNKIN

PUMPKIN

WATERMILLION WATERMELON

Noah spoke to merchants and war heroes, farmers and booksellers. "*Now* is the time, and *this* the country," he said.

But after eight years of war, people had no patience for changing the alphabet every which way. They just wanted life to return to normal.

Noah soon realized that even Ben couldn't make people accept new letters.
A new alphabet was even more inconvenient than the old one.
While his friend labored over the Constitution, an idea stirred in Noah's mind.
What if they didn't change the alphabet?

Armed with the twenty-six letters of the English alphabet everyone knew and loved, Noah launched a spelling revolution—ready to turn "rong" spelling into "rite."

OUT with
silent letters

THUMB

ISLAND

HAVE

ONE vowel
for short sounds

HEAD→HED

TWO for long!

SEAT→SEET

OUT with
unnecessary
extras!

SPELL

MUSICK

HONOUR

ONE sound for each letter!

NO confusion!

Free at last from the King's
English with its unreliable rules!

From north to south and east to
west, all citizens would spell the
same and speak the same! The
states would truly be *united*!

In city after city, Noah appealed to writers and printers, schoolmasters and penny-pinchers. Without extra letters they'd save time, save paper, save money! Children could learn to read and write in one year instead of four!

He answered questions, explained every detail. Old meanings and spellings didn't matter. "Was 'peace' ever mistaken for 'piece'; 'pray' for 'prey'; 'flour' for 'flower'? Never . . . no inconvenience," Noah said. Good spellers could learn in a week. Poor spellers could rejoice; they were already doing it right.

Ben studied Noah's plan. "Excellent work," he wrote. Old and ailing, Ben still believed in making reading and writing easier. He still believed in spelling changes. He still believed in Noah.

When Ben died in 1790, Noah carried on, trying out new spellings with the public.

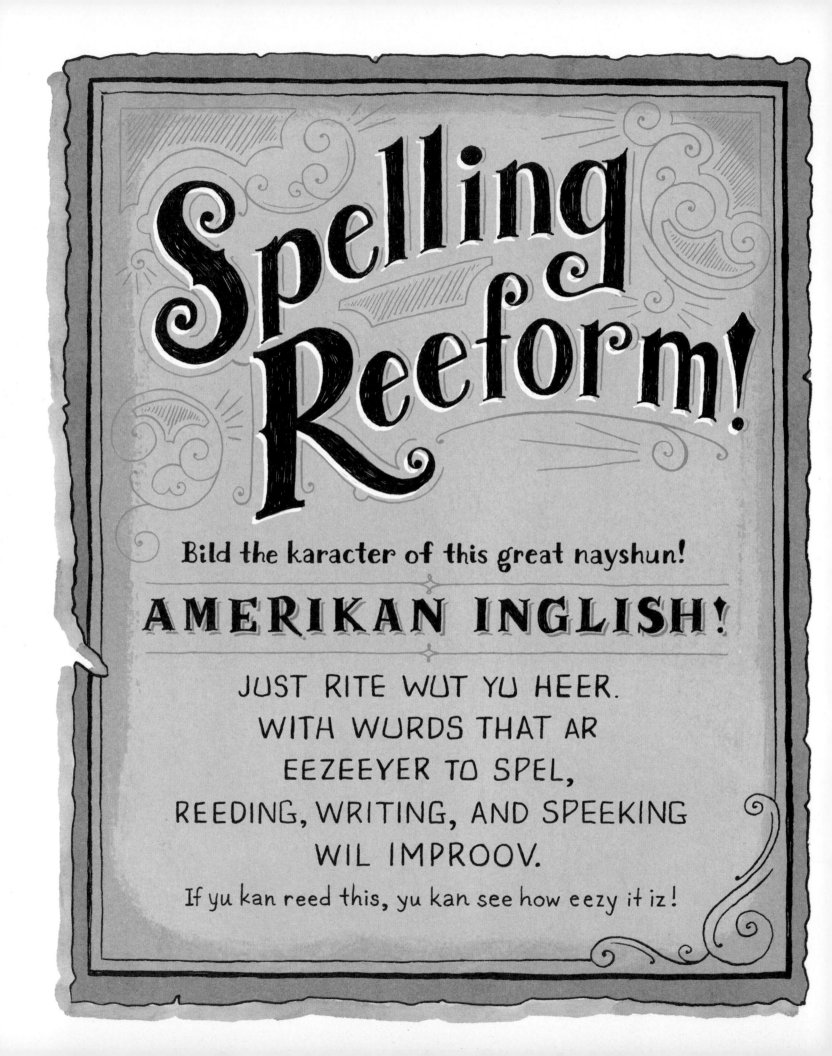

As you know, sometimes what appears to be easy can turn out to be hard. Noah understood. Too many changes. He forged ahead.

PLAN C

Noah focused on one change—drop silent letters.

Simple, sensible, only slightly inconvenient.

Newspapermen began to use new spellings.

THE DAILY NEWS

HONORED TO USE WEBSTER'S NEW SPELLINGS

BLUE IS A GREAT COLOR

Authors refused.

I shall go to live on a deserted ISLAND before I shall use Webster's new spellings

Neither mattered. Because American people were unwilling to change old habits, unwilling to be bothered, unwilling to take liberties with their language.

But Noah was getting closer.
As the spelling revolution faded,
a new idea stirred in his mind.

A dictionary . . . an *American* dictionary! With the country's new words. New meanings. And, yes . . . some new spellings.

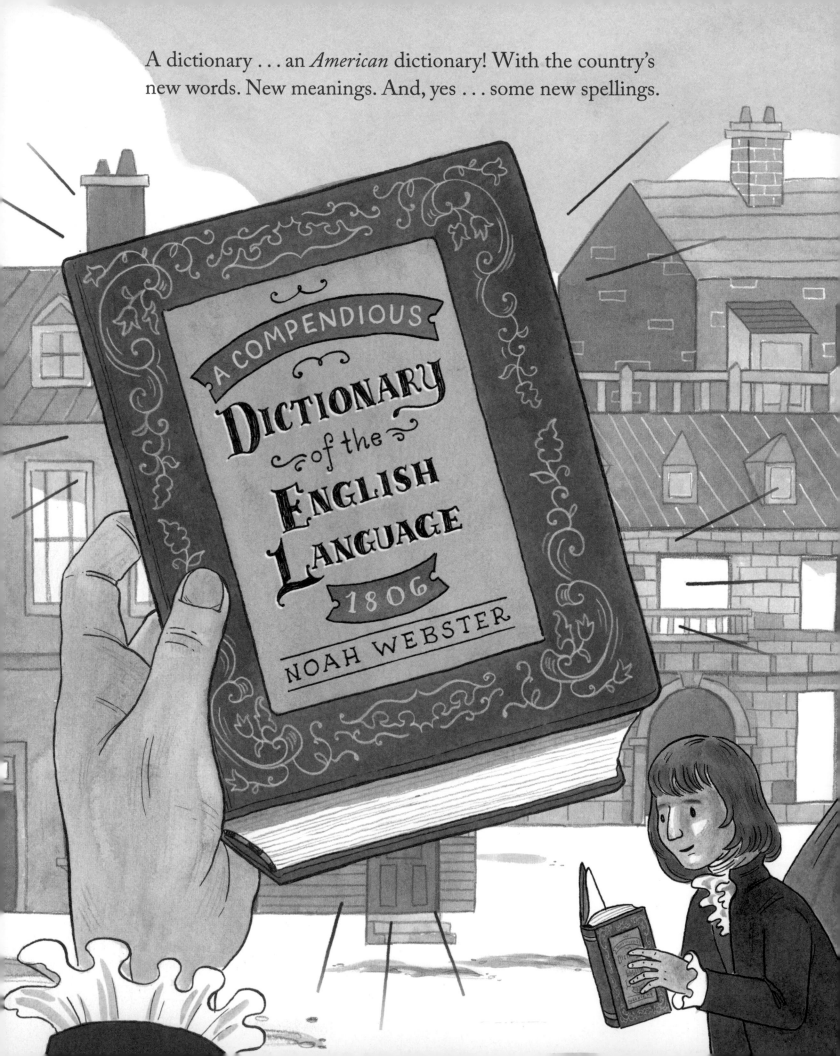

Noah read and researched, wrote and revised. In 1806, he published his first dictionary with 37,000 words. And like his old friend Ben, Noah let his idea take its chance in the world.

Americans from north to south and east to west began to use the same English. Noah kept on. Twenty-two years later, his *American Dictionary of the English Language* boasted 70,000 words.

Today, American dictionaries include many of Noah's
spelling changes and thousands upon thousands
of new words—all spelled with the same old
inconvenient alphabet:
Letters with too many sounds.
Sounds with too many letters.
And some letters just not needed at all.

Next time you sound out a word,
think of Ben and Noah.

THAY WUD BEE
PLEEZ'D
BEECUZ THAT
IZ EGZAKTLEE WUT
THAY WONTED!

*"Those people spell best
who do not know how to spell."*

—Benjamin Franklin

A Note from the Author

As I worked on this story, I was reminded of a moment in fifth grade. I had been writing with all my heart, pouring words onto the paper. When I reread my work, I found that I had spelled "of" *u-v*. I was shocked. Really, "uv"? I had known how to spell "of" for years. How embarrassing! What was I thinking? Well, I guess I wasn't thinking—about spelling. My brain was immersed in writing, and it let my hand do what made sense. That just might have been the moment my fascination with this crazy language, English, began.

Since then, technology has changed writing. If I typed "uv" today, a red line would tell me to check the spelling.

If Ben and Noah could see us now, I wonder what they'd think of computers and texting. Surely they'd be amazed by spell-check. But even spell-check isn't perfect. With so many sound-alike words in English, we still must determine if a word is the

right/write/rite/wright

one/won

for/four/fore

the sentence.

Which is, unfortunately, a little inconvenient.

Both Ben and Noah were dedicated to improving and providing universal education for American children. As Noah Webster said, "The only practicable method to reform mankind is to begin with children. Education should therefore be the first care of a legislature."

Ben Franklin died in 1790, leaving a legacy of inventions, discoveries, and political leadership that changed life in America. While we might be familiar with many of his successes, we seldom hear of his failures. Certainly, he had many on his way to his accomplishments. As he said, "Energy and persistence conquer all things."

Noah Webster slowly let many of the spelling changes go and returned to accepted forms for most words. He kept improving his schoolbook with new editions, selling more than 100 million copies over the years. While the spelling reform was not successful in the eye of the public, it was a stepping-stone for what really made Webster famous, the first truly American dictionary. With it, he was finally able to create a standard for English spelling and pronunciation. When Webster published his first dictionary in 1806, it included many new words, as well as some of the spelling changes that make American English different from British English. Some of the changes you will see today include *-our* endings that became *-or* (color, favor), *-re* endings that became *-er* (theater, center), *-ce* endings that became *-se* (defense), and *-ck* endings that dropped the *k* (music, public). Also "plough" is now "plow," "waggon" is "wagon," and "gaol" is "jail."

Even though writing systems may remain the same, languages are constantly transforming. Meanings change, old words are forgotten, and new words are borrowed or created. Pronunciation also changes, resulting in letters that no longer match sounds.

In English, the *ch* that sounds like *k* in "character" came from the Greeks; the silent *k* in "knot" came from the Vikings; and the *gh* in "light" came from the Anglo-Saxons. The history of words—etymology—is fascinating.

In Ben and Noah's time, American English had been adding new words for 150 years. From French and Spanish, German and Dutch. From Native American and African languages. With different sounds, from different alphabets. Colonists also made up words to describe plants and animals, farm life, foods, and the new frontier.

Today, English continues to change through everyday use as people create or borrow words they need to describe ideas, products, discoveries, and experiences. Recent additions include "emoji," "selfie," "fracking," "colossal squid," "Seussian," and "air ball." Each year the Merriam-Webster dictionary adds more than one thousand new words.

Since Ben and Noah's attempt, others have tried to reform spelling. As you can see by the words on the page, they, too, were unsuccessful.

Why do you think it is so hard to change?

A Few Notes on the Research

Ben Franklin's original writings include letters he wrote sharing his new alphabet with a friend (who criticized it) and his sister (who praised it). Though we know he printed a pamphlet explaining his plan, it is unknown how many other people saw his proposal.

Unfortunately, the details of "Plan A," Ben and Noah's collaboration that included a new alphabet, have been lost to history. There is no way of knowing whether Webster included Franklin's new symbols.

In this book, the principles of Ben Franklin and Noah Webster's spelling reform were simplified and applied to today's standard pronunciation in a manner that would allow young people to read the phonetic spelling.

While most sources say that American English has forty-four sounds, the number may vary slightly depending upon dialect. Today, we still hear accents in different parts of the United States, but they seldom cause misunderstanding. Instead, these language differences add character and culture to our diverse land.

A Note from the Illustrator

As far as I am aware, neither Ben Franklin nor Noah Webster owned any pets. So what's the deal with the cat and dog "sidekicks" you see throughout the book? There are a couple of reasons for this. First of all, while it is very proper and appropriate to learn about history from two men wearing tights and ponytails, it can be a little tiresome to only see drawings of them throughout the entirety of the book. I drew Ben a total of twenty-four times and Noah twenty-six times! The dog and cat step in from time to time to help move the story along and to take some of the pressure off our main characters. Secondly, I thought that the young scrappy pup and wise older cat were great representations of Ben's and Noah's personalities. Noah's dog was inspired by my own dog, a Boston terrier named Franklin (funnily enough). He's young, full of energy, and always on the go—just like Noah. Ben's cat is a combination of my two cats, Penny and Harry. They are much older, wiser, and a bit calmer, but still are curious and eager to learn—just like Ben. And lastly, I love animals and try to sneak them into my drawings whenever possible. They make me laugh, and I hope they make you smile too!

Quotation Sources

"to take their chance in the world" (Franklin and Sparks, *The Works of Benjamin Franklin*, 344.)

"converse together like children of the same family" (Webster, *Dissertations on the English Language*, 36.)

"*Now* is the time, and *this* the country" (Webster, *Dissertations on the English Language*, 551.)

"Was peace ever mistaken for piece; pray for prey; flour for flower? Never . . . no inconvenience" (Webster, *Dissertations on the English Language*, 546.)

"Excellent work" (Kendall, *The Forgotten Founding Father*, 149.)

"Those people spell best who do not know how to spell" (Melis, *Noah Webster and the First American Dictionary*, 102.)

"The only practicable method . . ." (Unger, *Noah Webster*, 142.)

"Energy and persistence conquer all things" (Franklin, *Quotations of Benjamin Franklin*, 22.)

BIBLIOGRAPHY

Primary Sources

Franklin, Benjamin. *The Autobiography of Benjamin Franklin.* New York: Buccaneer Books, 1984. Print.

———. *Quotations of Benjamin Franklin.* Vol. 1. Bedford, MA: Applewood, 2003. Print.

Franklin, Benjamin, and William Temple Franklin. *The Private Correspondence of Benjamin Franklin . . . Comprising a Series of Letters on Miscellaneous, Literary, and Political Subjects: Written Between the Years 1753 and 1790; Illustrating the Memoirs of His Public and Private Life, and Developing the Secret History of His Political Transactions and Negociations. Published from the Originals, by His Grandson William Temple Franklin.* Vol. 1, 3rd ed. London: Printed for H. Colburn, 1818. (Original University of Michigan.) Google Books, accessed 29 Jan. 2016. Web.

———. *The Private Correspondence of Benjamin Franklin.* Vol. 2. London: Printed for H. Colburn, 1833. (Original New York Public Library.) Google Books, accessed 29 Jan. 2016. Web.

Franklin, Benjamin, and Jared Sparks. "A Scheme for a New Alphabet and Reformed Mode of Spelling." *The Works of Benjamin Franklin: Containing Several Political and Historical Tracts Not Included in Any Former Edition, and Many Letters Official and Private Not Hitherto Published: With Notes and a Life of the Author.* Vol. 6. Boston: Hilliard, Gray & Company, 1840, pp. 295–303. (Original Stanford University Library.) Google Books, accessed 29 Jan. 2016. Web.

Franklin, Benjamin, and Benjamin Vaughan. *Political, Miscellaneous, and Philosophical Pieces: Arranged Under the Following Heads, and Distinguished by Initial Letters in Each Leaf: [G. P.] General Politics; [A. B. T.] American Politics Before the Troubles; [A. D. T.] American Politics During the Troubles; [P. P.] Provincial or Colony Politics; and [M. P.] Miscellaneous and Philosophical Pieces.* London: Printed for J. Johnson, 1779, pp. 467–78. (Original New York Public Library.) Google Books, accessed 29 Jan. 2016. Web.

Packard Humanities Institute. *The Papers of Benjamin Franklin.* (Original Yale University.) Franklinpapers.org, accessed 23 Mar. 2016. Web.

Webster, Noah. *The American Spelling Book: Containing an Easy Standard of Pronunciation. Being the First Part of a Grammatical Institute of the English Language.* 7th ed. Boston: I. Thomas and E. T. Andrews, 1793. Google Books, accessed 31 Jan. 2016. Web.

———. *A Collection of Essays and Fugitiv Writings: On Moral, Historical, Political, and Literary Subjects.* Boston: I. Thomas and E. T. Andrews, 1790.

———. *Dissertations on the English Language: With Notes Historical and Critical. To Which Is Added by Way of Appendix, An Essay on a Reformed Mode of Spelling, with Dr. Franklin's Arguments on That Subject.* Boston: I. Thomas and Company, 1789.

———. *Letters of Noah Webster,* ed. Harry R. Warfel. New York: Library Publishers, 1953. Print.

———. *Sketches of American Policy,* ed. Harry R. Warfel. New York: Scholars' Facsimiles & Reprints, 1937. Print.

Webster, Noah, and Richard M. Rollins. *The Autobiographies of Noah Webster: From the Letters and Essays, Memoir, and Diary.* Columbia, SC: University of South Carolina, 1989. Print.

Secondary Sources

"Background Research Notes: CODE REFORM (ATTEMPTS) HISTORY." Childrenofthecode.org (under "Benjamin Franklin" and "Noah Webster" listings), accessed 29 Jan. 2016. Web.

Blake, Norman Francis, Roger Lass, and John Algeo. *The Cambridge History of the English Language.* Vol. 6. Cambridge University Press, 2001. Google Books, accessed 9 Mar. 2016. Web.

Bryson, Bill. *The Mother Tongue: English and How It Got That Way.* New York: HarperCollins, 2001. Print.

Kendall, Joshua. *The Forgotten Founding Father: Noah Webster's Obsession and the Creation of an American Culture.* New York: G. P. Putnam's Sons, 2011. Print.

Lepore, Jill. *A Is for American: Letters and Other Characters in the Newly United States.* New York: Alfred A. Knopf, 2002. Print.

Melis, Luisanna Fodde. *Noah Webster and the First American Dictionary.* New York: PowerPlus, 2005. Print.

Mencken, H. L. *The American Language: An Inquiry into the Development of English in the United States.* 2nd ed. New York: A. A. Knopf, 1921. (Original University of Michigan.) Google Books, accessed 24 Mar. 2016. Web.

Micklethwait, David. *Noah Webster and the American Dictionary.* Jefferson, NC: McFarland, 2000. Print.

Noah Webster House & West Hartford Historical Society. "Noah Webster History." Noahwebsterhouse.org, accessed 17 Sept. 2016. Web.

Pearson, Ellen Holmes. "The Standardization of American English." Teachinghistory.org, accessed 29 Jan. 2016. Web.

Robinson, Sal. "Benjamin Franklin's Phonetic Alphabet and the Development of American English." Melville House Books, 25 July 2013. Mhpbooks.com, accessed 29 Jan. 2016. Web.

Skeel, Emily Ellsworth Ford. *Notes on the Life of Noah Webster.* Vol. 1. New York: Privately printed, 1912. (Original University of Michigan.) Google Books, accessed 1 Feb. 2016. Web.

Snyder, K. Alan. *Defining Noah Webster: A Spiritual Biography.* Fairfax, VA: Allegiance Press, 2002. Google Books, accessed 21 Aug. 2016. Web.

Twilley, Nicola. "Six New Letters for a Reformed Alphabet." At http://www.benfranklin300.org/_etc_pdf/Six_New_Letters_Nicola_Twilly.pdf, accessed 10 Mar. 2016. Web.

Unger, Harlow G. *Noah Webster: The Life and Times of an American Patriot.* New York: John Wiley & Sons, 1998. Print.

"Webster's Dictionary." *Old Dominion: A Monthly Magazine of Literature, Science, and Art,* vol. 6 (1872): 81–94. (Original Princeton University.) Google Books, accessed 25 Mar. 2016. Web.